Missing the Owl

Missing the Owl

poems by Richard Widerkehr

SHANTI ARTS PUBLISHING

BRUNSWICK, MAINE

Missing the Owl

Published by Shanti Arts Publishing

Designed by Shanti Arts Designs

Cover image by Linda Ford, September 4, 2024; used with her
permission.

Shanti Arts LLC
193 Hillside Road
Brunswick, Maine 04011
shantiarts.com

Printed in the United States of America

All poems about patients on 4-South are fictional, and 4-South
is a fictional place.

Ariel, Caliban, and Prospero are characters in Shakespeare's
The Tempest. Prospero is a magician; Caliban is his slave,
the son of a witch; and Ariel is a spirit who performs
"rough magic," sometimes unwillingly, for his master.

ISBN: 978-1-962082-45-7 (softcover)

Library of Congress Control Number (LCCN): 2024949649

for Linda

Contents

Missing the Owl

Acknowledgments

Adventures Northwest: "In the Forest, There Are Stars"

Atlanta Review: "What If Lot's Two Married Daughters Had Survived: Forty Years Later"

Bellingham Review: "Climbing the Air: Caliban Speaks"

Blueline: "Elegy with Two Placards on a Goat Shed" and "Under the Dock"

Cathexis Northwest Press: "At Akumal"; "The Judder"; and "Rungs of Air"

Cirque: "As We Walk West on Dupont Street"

Crab Creek Review: "Night Watchman's Afternoon" and "Red Curtains"

Crack The Spine: "January 6, 2021"

Door Is a Jar: "High School Graduation Swing-Out"; "A Holding Action"; "In the Lobby Bar at Akumal"; and "Near Whatcom Falls in Late September"

Ekphrastic Review: "In Our Grandma Hale's Painting, Which She Gave Me" and "Morning Light"

I-70 Review: "Messenger in Early November"

The Main Street Rag: "American Sentences"; "Migration: You Ask Me What I Want"; "Missing The Owl"; "On Our Thirty-Fifth Anniversary"; and "Wildfires, St. Paul Riots"

Measure: "Ariel Released"

Muse/A Journal: "Metamorphosis: Isabel Speaks"

Natural Bridge: "When She Was a Mermaid"

Naugatuck River Review: "Don't Be Alone with Her, The Charge Nurse Will Tell Ira"

Open: A Journal of Arts & Letters: "In Our Grandma Hale's Painting, Which She Gave Me"; "Spin the Bottle"; "Sympathy for the Scarecrow"; "When a Hawk Flushes an Undulating Flock of Dunlins"; and "When You Ask about That Dream"

Pennine Ink: "I, Isaac, Son of Sarah" and "Miracle Time"

Poetry Quarterly: "Stone Rooms: Ira Speaks"

Psaltery & Lyre: "Saying Evening Prayers at Zoom Services"

Shot Glass Journal: "Other Duties as Assigned" and "Three-Day Power Outage"

Sweet Tree Review: "At the Laidla Restaurant"; "Fable"; "In the Forest, There Are Stars"; "In the Lobby Bar at Akumal"; and "One of These Days"

Third Wednesday: "My Move"

West Trade Review: "The Other Life"

"If I put down the thing I saw and enjoyed, it would not give me the kind of feeling it gave me. I had to create an equivalent for what I felt I was looking at."

—Georgia O'Keeffe

Sympathy for the Scarecrow

When You Ask about That Dream

I'm lost in Yakima, but it's more like New York.
As I trudge through abandoned buildings,
looking for my dog Zach, dead two years now,
things seem familiar, like a city
where I lost something—ashes,
a few small, cold stars. A woman I don't know
follows me through vestibules and alcoves
whose mailboxes have been jimmied out.
We heave open a wrought-iron door.
Zach hauls himself up when he sees me,
his fur matted, his body thin.
Absently, slowly, we walk down the street
as we did when the tumor
had weakened him. I hear a thud
and turn. Near a rusty burn barrel,
Zach's lying in a hole in the ground.
I bend to help him. Low flames
lick at his fur, flicker down his side.
I pat at beige and brown patches
almost smoldering, put my arms around him,
feeling the strength across his chest—
this fallen king, a god in disguise,
who used to lie at my door
like a sleepy lion, who butted his head
into my lap when I worked at the typewriter,
who came whenever I asked.

At Akumal, Mexico

A green iguana guards its crevice,
claws splayed in sand by the rock face.
Basking, it slits its eyes at the sun,
a god with no animal sorrow.

Thirsty, I stand in the heat, inspecting
the lizard's blunt head, its shoulders
nearly one third its body. Stripes of ash,
green-gray, black, down its sides.

Strings of mist kiss the reef.
When the iguana's mate skitters
out, its hinged jaw juts up.
By the swinging arms of water,

he sips from a beaker,
the sun's urn of sleep—
its lips with many mouths.

White clouds do almost nothing.

The Judder

The judder is a ship's silhouette seen through the distortion of turbulent air off water; androgen deprivation therapy is used by men with prostate cancer that recurs after surgery and radiation.

At Akumal, this black ferry in sun glare
almost wobbles on the horizon, and the judder
blurs, as if two sister ships had met. As kids
we asked questions like *If you had to pick,*

would you rather lose your arms or your legs?
Now my oncologist says, *You may be able*
to have sex. Emotions? More like your wife's.
Evenings by the fireplace, our tiger-striped

cat on my lap—how the root of the Hebrew
word for *sacrifice* means *to draw close.*
Now the judder, two silhouettes not dissevered—
how the root of our word *decision* means *cut.*

Red Curtains

In her sunny room, the dust motes
went up like curtain ropes, as the hum
of the air conditioner mixed with
too much Pernod. She was taking off
her dress, letting it fall
on the table next to the plate of oranges
and the picture of her husband
and the kids. Separated three months,
she never talked about them, and I
didn't ask. The first time we made love
happened fast. The next time,
her cries got higher, and mine
got closer to hers, caught up with the columns
in the dusty air, a red sun
floating in the afterglow. As we rested,
I saw our bodies were made of
red sand.
        Six months later, she left.
I thought of the night her daughter
slept over, sounds of her low breathing
coming from the darkened
living room.

Now as I walk into the city,
crowds of people with bodies made of
wet wool and eyes like dirty snow
assemble and reassemble. I see my face
in subway windows, mirrors
I was meant to look in, having refused
or been afraid to admit
I loved her then.

In the Lobby Bar at Akumal

Abuelo means *grandfather.*

Under the latticework of thatch and wood, a young woman
pulls me onto the floor. *You're dancing with me,*
she says. I've been Lindy stepping in the shadows.
Now our bodies sway to "Chain Of Fools." Maybe,
a light box has stolen bits of the yellow super moon,
spilled them on black water.
                              Her tight black jeans,
her black eyes—is she thinking, *Don't want to give
this abeulo a heart attack?* The almost-full moon,
pieces of eight on ink-spot waves. I'm smoke in smoke;
she's fire in fire.

Wildfires in August, Three-Day Power Outage

Wind tore trees from sidewalks—so we read by flashlight,
remember all the dry leaves in the heat, evenings
when the sun hung in the smoke like diesel.
In the dark, we think we saw

the striped hawk moth affixed
one day to our screen door by the slate steps
like a messenger; yellow-jackets fumbling
at our sills, as if half-asleep;

the big-leaf maples, once green-gold,
now tangled, diehard lovers.
The blue smudge that hung over the lake
like a halo—it wasn't a sign, was it?

Oh, we know which candles must be lit,
as rain hits the cracked, black earth.

Rungs of Air

After reading your email, "You Are My High School Memory," I receive
external beam radiation under a Calypso 4D Localization System.

I can't tell you much about this table—a scanner
shows the Calypso tech where to beam Xray slices.
You won't glow, said the nurse. *Just don't go*

through airport security. The margins of sunlight,
of stories? *Your surgical margins negative,*
that's a plus. My mother said you had cat eyes,

a Day-Glo green almost feral, skittish. Our bodies
two refrigerators burning. Now I ask for daily magic,
a moth affixed to a screen door—your pixels

on my screen, surnames of thirst, full-body scans.
When I sang "Puff, the Magic Dragon" for my mother,
she said, *Keep singing*, scanned windows

for the black cat. *A leaky boat*
don't owe you anything, kiddo. The margins
down, the markets up, then crashing.

You were fire fascinated with itself:
More air, more air, you said. As for that sheen
of burning gasoline, your magic,

stones and stories, margins starry
and omniscient—you ran down the stairs.
Now a voice says, *Stay still.*

Calypso's rasp and buzz. I cannot climb
rungs of air. Linda's the air I breathe.
Gentle and sweet you said I was.

Under the Dock

—*in memory of our father*

1

Under a snow-capped pier on pale, bright water,
his shadow steps off the edge.

2

Gold leaves in October, ashen bark, that sky of indigo
not yet fallen.

3

Twilit water. On the horizon, a line of light;
we can't see him.

Near Whatcom Falls in Late September

—in memory of J. W.

At last this big-leaf maple on my path,
red and ochre. At last low waves
on the sides of black rocks. I pick up a leaf,
crush its pale, scarlet tent

to my lips. Allegedly, she took her life—
her body, *they sprinted it away*,
you tell me. Sun on sandstone
ledges and gray lichen.

I turn the stem in my fingers;
the leaf shimmers, rocks in the light.
White bodies of water falling—
I thought she was fire.

One of These Days

The trees are going to walk out of their world
into ours. They'll see how we get peevish
after a succession of sunny days, how we
ask God for explanations, or an excuse.

The trees, which give us everything—
their light, leaves, shadows in the sun—
what will they say when we show them
staircases, our houses that can't see the sky?

Must we tell them how sometimes
we grow harsh in our search for meaning
and beauty? Not to mention how we

cut thousands of board-feet of lumber
and, like a generalissimo, light cigars
on the first rainy day.

Elegy with Two Placards on a Goat Shed

In the Talmud it says we should live as if we have a piece of paper
which on one side says, "I am dust and ashes"; and on the other side,
"This world was created for me."

> *—in memory of S. O.*

That August you helped Linda plant a bed of native plants
near these geometric star bursts, yellow-and-red
quilt patterns not far from our goat pasture—
the goats long gone, the shed a ramshackle habitat
for Douglas squirrels and white-crowned sparrows.

As I worked on my lines about smoggy skies
back East, childhood's long fly balls at twilight
suspended in mid-air—*memoir is reverie, a sieve,*
I wrote—you worked in the sun, yanked out bindweed,
hacked at blackberry tangles near the woods

where trillium almost hid the Hooker's Fairy Bells.
Now two black-cowled towhees peck at seeds
under the feeder, shuttle back and forth to the shed.
Unlike ravens that wait, albeit croaking, or the crows
with their flak of scratchy, *ack-ack* clauses,

I do not say your name. No cloak of dust
and ashes at my throat, just the other side
of a Talmud boy's smudged piece of paper
in my pocket. At the end, did you ask,
Was this world created for us?

At the Laidla Restaurant
after External Beam Radiation

In the tapestry over our corner table, black-and-white clouds
in moonlight—a woman in crimson plucks her harp.
As I lay on a table in the Infinity Room
under a Calypso 4-D localization system,
my doctor said, *Drink lots of water.* In this tapestry,
red pleats and creases, the swell of the woman's belly—
cloud lines follow notes and scrolls her fingers
have unfolded. *What is it?* asks Linda.
We have no son, no daughter.

In the Forest, There Are Stars

Thick green-black branches can't hide them,
whistling through cedar and fir trees. You've seen
one star drop as if torn from the forest.

Here stars jostle each other, falling toward you—
you forget what you were and how you came here.
Maybe by day on the road to the islands,

can you remember, the white edges
of rooftops, how the forest rose to meet you?
Here sword ferns jut from the hillsides.

High fern-like branches fan themselves downward,
and stars soak you with their cold radiance.
The stars that were small and cold

in the sky are still small and cold. The branches
lift about them, hissing lightly.

Sympathy for the Scarecrow

What's wrong—why can't he free his arms,
call on beasts of mercy? As if he must appease
the gods of flame and so forth, amp up
his adrenaline and dread, he flails his spindly

limbs in the wind. The crows on topsoil
by the new starts know this isn't just work.
No one texts him, sends a video, reminds him
of the last time he walked on fire.

Shall we discuss his mute, charred eyes,
or leave that to the guardians of straw?
He gazes at the center of the blue spruce,

as if the trunk might see his ashen wrists,
fluent as wings once more as promised,
burning, of course, like dead bees.

Spin the Bottle

I remember the front closet in the dim foyer
of Deena Mitzfeld's place in Forest Hills,
which had no forest and a few hills. The bottle
we spun had pointed to my toes, her toes, her knees
encased in white knee socks with a blue stripe.
In the rummage sale of shadows in her closet,
we kissed like minnows. The brush of her lips—
no, it wasn't nothing, but what was it?

I can't recall the smell of her hair, whether
our fingers touched. Almost as if our bodies
were off in Bakersfield—her father's suit coats
could have been zoot suits for all I knew, and her
mom's frocks—did I even know the word *frock?*
We said nothing, as if we were suppliants
fated to enact this ritual of coats and shadows,
tacit witnesses who, if they saw us, had the tact

to say nothing. As we two were fated never
to say word one about our—well, it was *my*
first kiss. I don't recall what floor of that brick
monolith Deena's parents' apartment was on,
only that the living room window looked out
on a jungle gym in the tentative playground
where next day I would hold out my arms,
a paper airplane with no regrets, and fly.

Climbing the Air

In the Hall of North American Mammals:
Museum of Natural History

Writing in the cool of the morning near the diorama
of the saber-toothed tiger—
no need to tell you about my tar pit of an apartment
near the river in Manhattan or the nettles I fell in when I fled
to Day Creek.

You don't want a woman, said the hooker
in red hot pants in Times Square. In the summer of love,
nights in Adam & Eve's,
I nursed Stingers 'cause that's what Bogart drank.
And yet,
under my Vodka-and-burnt-toast breath,

I muttered, *God, please take my life.*

In the cool of the morning, the frozen saber tooth
beige-gold. Sometimes, yes, I soared
like a god with his female city
in air, in fog with its/her orange-pink halo
at night over the Empire State Building,
the spire King Kong fell from,
his fist uncurling, fingers letting go,
setting down Fay Wray slowly,
tenderly,
at dawn, on her ice-gray platform,
not calling *God God*

Her Jack-Knife

Our summer began with Asra's jack-knife
off the diving board at the lake on Indian Memorial Drive.
How she stepped backwards off the board in her yellow two-piece,
tucked in her arms, knees, touched her toes—
her tan, compact body straightened, and she dove
through the clean space in air she had created.
Hardly any splash. "Nice dive," I said.

I practiced somersaults in shallow water, learned to do a forward
one-and-a-half, though bumped my head once on the board.
At the center of the lake, we kissed underwater, our lips pressed
together like two minnows. Now, she writes, the fireweed has gone
white. Brown, crumpled cups of Queen Anne's Lace at the lake.
The Woolworth ring I gave her, she almost lost in Red River.

On Sunday, I will ride my bike on the shoulder
of the Long Island Expressway to the Whitestone Bridge,
then up the thruway. We went skinny dipping one night.
She let me look. Now there's this song on the radio,
"See You in September." What I hear is *summer, summer.*

I, Isaac, Son of Sarah

The moon is a hole in the night
in the dream I will have
of this mountain—my father
has me gather kindling, binds me

with cords of twisted linen.
Where is the ram for the sacrifice?
I ask. In his sleep he has named
other gods who feast their thirst

ten times mere marrow. *The Lord
will provide the ram*, he says.
His fixed eyes lusterless, my father

unwraps his flint, unsheathes the knife.
The moon a hole in God's good eye—
I whose name means *laughter.*

Miracle Time

Kneeling by the water's edge, she looks for shells.
Sun lights the down on the small of her back. In the water,
shadows float over her image. All morning
she's picked up white shells, set them down—
when he speaks, she doesn't answer.

Now she pushes off into the still water.
Her long hair trails behind her. Reaching the sandbar,
she crosses to the other side, crouches,
picks up a shell, puts it back down,
while with the other hand she wrings the water
out of her fist in bursts.
                            All at once, she turns
from the waist only and smiles like a woman
who knows he won't buy her a yellow straw hat
after they hitch rides on motorcycles
to St. Armand's Key—maybe, she knows
how the sun will open in spokes
over the swing-set near Division Street
and she'll say Miracle Time, and he
won't ask her to marry him.

Biloxi

When I fainted in the heat at the bake sale in Biloxi where
I had taken a break from selling World Books door to door,
she called 911. I awoke, my face in her lap, scent of musk
and violets, her hands crossed over one bare leg slung idly
across a green, stuffed armchair. Sirens. Porch swings. Two
shattered statues of red roosters. Twelve cradles. Why was
I counting her things? When I put my hand in her cookie jar,
she slapped my face, then said, "I shouldn't have done that."
First Aid told me, "Stay out of the sun. You cannot afford
even one of her twelve broken electrical circuits, not one
cradle." I was done with encyclopedias, rosters of unsold
books. What were these smoke signals on the ridge called
Autanum? As I squinted at one scarab insect on her gold
screen door, I knew I would not become an accountant like
my father. Why was I singing "Home on the Range?"

Ariel Released

His last day on the island, Prospero said
to follow him where sea stacks guard the sea.
Under one arm, he lugged his magic book,
climbing the broken shore. From a high stand
overlooking the island's point, he stared
at the horizon. When he shook his head,
the sea grew wild. I feared he'd never set
me free. Wind stung our faces with fine spray
shaken from basalt caves that clenched and ground
as wave after wave fell on the steep shore.
When had they wished for loss of majesty?
He stood above them on the jutting height
and seemed no different. Nothing changed his gaze.
But all at once, he knelt down and released
his book like breath into the ocean's jaw.
I guessed he thought it was the proper way.
At last, he stood up. Leaning on one leg,
he clutched his sleeve. For the first time, his eyes
were scored with crooked veins. When I looked down,
he told me I was free. I felt the wind
push in around me. Tears came to my eyes.
I asked to walk with him at least to where
the shoreline bends, but he said no. Was I
ungrateful to him? Did I condescend?
I hadn't thought to hope he'd set me free.
And so I'm free. Often I think of times
his magic turned the world into a stage,
and I watched by his side, or tricked a fool,
arranged a masque, saw to the tempest, told

him what came next when he forgot. I was
important. Now I often find myself
alone, here on the human shore. The island
is mine. The waves resume their punishment.
I wonder if Prospero's new life is good,

if it's been worth it after all, and if
he left me here on purpose. Caliban,
the monster, hankers for a god to serve
again. He walks, sighing among the trees,
and nothing answers. Sometimes when the night
is cold, I think he might do worse than choose
me for his god. But Prospero's image stays
with me like years. I think of him with head thrust
back and eyes fixed on the sea's flat rim.
For till he unlocked all our bondages,
wasn't my master yearning to be free?

Climbing the Air: Caliban Speaks

I saw her walking softly in a field
of yellow corn, parting the stalks. Her hands
let light in. All the ranks quickened to yield.
None thought of warding off her soft commands.
Perhaps, she saw me staring by the fence,
for she leaned her face into the faint breeze
and turned the other way, seeming to sense,
not see, the wavering shafts. The awful ease
she moved with made me want to run and tear
the fence posts up and hurl them in a ring.
But when I called her name and climbed the air,
trampling the stalks to run and do the thing,
her eyes were more disdainful than surprised.
All that I wanted. All that I despised.

Night Watchman's Afternoon

There may be losses too great to understand that rove after you and—
faint and terrible—rip unknown through your hand. —William Stafford

This joy in waking after long sleep
filled with dreams comes slowly—
the afternoon light sifts
coldly through the level blinds.
Just to lie thinking of wet lawns,
walks at night in rain—her white dress
half-undone in the driveway near the steps—
raises me on one elbow.

She's gone; now I wait.
As light drains through the blinds
from row houses up the street,
it lets me in on its thoughts.
The cold light tells me, *Keep threads,*
strands of air. If we meet between these blinds,
we won't speak. I'll kiss you
with my lips of wind. You won't reply.

I've lived in rooms of falling light; they close in
day by day. Light lies in pools, in doorways,
on the table's face. Last night
I worked my shift. Today as I slept,
the light explained things—someone leaving
cigarette burns on the windowsill, letting the phone ring.
The light went on: *Here houses have no walls.*

Some boxes are marked Sanctuary;
others are marked Grief. Watchman,
am I yours? I woke, weeping. Now I keep
closing and closing my eyes.

But at my table, joy sits
smoothing the oilcloth, fingering the blinds.
Tentative, she tells me
that she exists, that she experiences
my relief—asks for toast, sweet tea,
all the fixings. She says
she likes to smooth my wrinkles
with her spoon. Sweet joy,
let's pull the blinds. Let's eat.

When She Was a Mermaid

For him I keep popping up, as if I hadn't let slip
my jade heart on a chain, closed it in his hand.
For him, the clasp of my goodbye—did I mean
Run after me? or *Keep running?* For him
my silver chain, that net of luck and sorrow,
torn and mended like a witch's heart,
hungry for what *he'll* never . . .
Oh, let him keep the smell of bull-neck kelp.
If he doesn't sleep with the moon
in a cardboard box, at least he'll say my name.

Metamorphosis: Isabel Speaks

We no longer ask, How can a woman turn
into this or that, as if some god had burned a while,
got on with his business, left us a creature

with eight slipshod limbs that waver. Not to say goodbye,
we part the dim sea grasses, see what happened. Wasn't there
a white lilac tree? Was I the warden's daughter,

and you hauled me from my slip, untied certain ribbons,
dragged me to the bottom of the sea? One word, three hearts—
you say I gave you too much power. Now these limbs

waver in the script of water, as folded light sifts down
through scrollwork, as if it were still fall and certain lies
weren't centuries. You with your ships and cities,

lord of here and after—we wait with synonyms
for water: *petal, kiss.* You say in the other life
I must have been a witch, a weird sister. No, my lips,

they turned into this beak, by your black hulls that sway
in gold halls of sea lettuce, in purple knobs of coral that enfold
and loll upside down, topsy-turncoat blue in the dark,

where ligatures come unbound, and we scuttle,
star suckers with no religion, lips with many mouths. Our eight
limbs, bastard kisses. Didn't you tell me, *Lie down*

with the Southern Keeled Octopus, Star Sucker Pygmy,
particularly fond of crabs? You say you miss me, but things happen,
and we're not the same. Yes, I'm scared of water.

Oh my one-time student of desire who masks his knowledge,
sips insomniac glasses of Maker's Mark—ask yourself,
If you had eight convoluted arms, white in white light,

red in red—if you had three hearts that let ink spill
from a funnel near your eyes, could you tell the difference
between a leaf, a frog fish—that kiss, this clasp of water?

Other Duties as Assigned

Wearing pale latex gloves, Ira dips a black metal comb
in his tin bowl of water, picks nits from Claudia's dull
hair still wet from the shower. In her hospital gown,
she sits in front of him on a blue plastic chair. The cops
found her unconscious on Holly Street, her sugar

levels too high. Claudia doesn't think she's diabetic,
happens to be paranoid. A sign downstairs in their lobby:
We do the healing work of Jesus Christ. He is Jewish.
His plastic I.D. tag *Behavioral Health Counselor*
badges him in and out of double doors.

At least his sister no longer hears voices, no longer
sleeps with the moon in a cardboard box. His latex
gloves flesh-colored, his metal comb, the flecks
and bits, half-sunken carapaces in clear water—
when he sets the comb beside his tin bowl
on the bright, gray carpet, Claudia says, *Thanks.*

Don't Be Alone with Her,
The Charge Nurse Will Tell Ira

Yes, she says, i'm that Ophelia, got no use for princelings,
hate their mommy, love their mommy, yes, i wanted
him to have me, could forget him better if he had,
thinks 'cause he sniffed around me, who's him,
merry hamster on his cell phone, Hamlet
in his celibate cell. Don't put that stethoscope
in ya ear, you with the keys, pretend to help me
now, help me later, i'm not signing any forms
in ya solarium—here's mummy berries, hat pins,
Vaseline and bees, my Harley's outside, Handlebars,
i know u wanna go downtown with me, u just
a pirate scared of water, don't know booty
from ya breakfast, by the way, don't forget
to put the toilet seat back down, i can launch
ninety missiles from my blondie dreadlocks, i *know*
i got delusions, that don't mean there ain't no
crow in the kitchen, no, i can't slow down,
i left my urine sample in ya fridge, don't sing
me sad-eyed ballads, lowlands low, u talking
country matters, *no more shall madrigal*, hey,
someone died in this room, he lugged the guts,
u look like him, another scourge of heaven
gonna save me? When's the last time
u put new strings on that guitar? Jet back
to ya nurse's station, hoard and hand out capsules,
tell Dr. Who i'm not taking any meds—look,
out my window, past the pleasure boats,
that black headland, it starts to move, cool, huh,

u see it, don't u, in the dark, oh, i loved him
like a brother, not a brother, the danger
he was in, my dad the warden with his pistol
told him stay away, but i snuck out, and like a sea
horse out of water, he blamed me, a Catholic girl,
i planned the rhythm, but he got the condom out,
by then the moment, no, not wheat and flame—
u don't be singing, *no more shall madrigal*
or dream undrown—tell ya ravens
carry him home, Lord.

You Never Get Full? Ira Asks a Young Man

At our nurse's station near the fish tank,
Sheldon leans back in the light, chug-a-lugs
a can of cold beef stew. Our charge nurse
makes an upchuck motion, one finger

in her mouth. *You're sick, man*, says Dee.
I know, he replies with a jocular grin.
I've handed him his blue box of belongings,
his can opener. The jagged lid a *Sharp*,

yes, but he's on zero violence precautions.
No, I never get full, he tells me. Three days
later, he dies in the E.R. from a stroke.

Sheldon weighed over five hundred pounds.
In our fish tank, the Mollies, the Tetras pulse
and glow, the air pump breathing, breathing.

Lanterns That Smelled Like Rain: Ira Speaks

You had been carrying her and carrying her.
Why were there lanterns?

Were her veins really the color of stars up close?
Why were you carrying these lanterns?

How come you could see through the skin of her back?
Was there any rain left in the world?

It seemed that by watching her sleep
you could capture her secrets.

When you awoke, you wanted to cut off your arms
to see if they would go on carrying her.

The Other Life

If life is one thing and then another...   —Kerren McCadden

When the violet-green swallow
wrapped itself around the striped hawk moth
like a scarf,

what set the moth apart? When a gas station
near a freight yard lit tracks
that crisscrossed at night,

a boy and his girlfriend hopped a freight train—
the tracks, cities of wind
that could never be incinerated.

The boy didn't know the difference
between rain and the smell of rain,
dust and summer.

Maybe, she wanted to get married,
said his father. What did *he* know about lanterns
that smelled like rain?

What if Lot's Two Married Daughters Had Survived: Forty Years Later

At times we see black trees at evening,
almost silent in the heat, the low sun
no longer a stain of rage and grief—
we remember the early apples,

bees in the bee boxes,
times we prayed for pinpricks of rain
on our faces. Our mother's unwept salt,
we are her daughters.

Stone Rooms: Ira

The wind says, *It is not permitted you enter this place*
without leaving an offering. Even if these white and pink-gray
cliffs with their tepee-shaped monoliths were not sacred,

you did not see how we burned Old Man Gloom.
When you compliment our costumes, you insult us.
Go ahead, read your book about pyroclastic flow,

boulders flying from black scatter cones, layers scoured
and scored, scooped and scalloped, as if praised by simple wind
and water. We know ash and lava were not welded.

This is where Kweele, god of heat, son of the sun,
stalks the rueful. About such spirits, it has been written,
"Nobody sees them in the daytime, except sometimes

when the sun is going down, partly visible.
They watch the sun, sometimes one color,
sometimes all colors. They watch the people."

I keep an eagle's scream beneath my breastbone. Once,
close to death, I leafed through my dictionary, eyes closed.
When my eyes opened, my fingers rested on the word,

hallelujah. Voices in rocks say, *Pick your way, if you can,*
into this slot canyon. You cannot see our hooded dancers
file along the cliffs, their down-turned faces,

this boy made of white stone, watching, his one eye swollen like an outcrop. In my book, I read: Pyroclasts are fragments spewed like bombs from the Jemez Volcanic Field six to seven

million years ago. Pyroclastic flow: hot gases blasting down slopes in an incandescent avalanche. Tent rocks: made of ash and tuff. Weathering may have followed vertical joints; volcanic fumes

may have risen through porous ash, cementing it.
I lower my eyes from pale, conical faces, ninety feet high.
So much time inside these runes—as if I'd glimpsed

the death of gods, caprocks balanced on white bodies, symmetrical yet ruined. I climb past lightning clans, snake lines, leached, frozen faces. One piece of porous tuff forewarns me:

When air reaches heartwood, it hollows the tree. A red mountain dreams a white valley. When you had everything, it was not enough. Like that dark son, Ishmael, you walked into this desert's arroyos,

dry washes, as if climbing back through convalescence. Flash floods carry off the unwary. I listen for thunder. Snake signs are lightning symbols. By a green river, black jetty-jacks. An eagle floats

over rimrock, stone rooms in the sky, its scream a cholla cactus made of ash. At twilight, in the plazas of cities, stone fountains say nothing, as male mourning doves utter weightless cries.

Fable

Under a sun that's hard to tell from the moon,
a man in an overcoat and fedora waits, hands in pockets.
He spots an egg-shaped stone,

which spills yellow light
onto a dirt path near the edge
of a stubble field.

The man's face, half-hidden beneath his gray hat—
he doesn't believe in ghosts. He likes to stand
on doorsills, thresholds,

clasping each moment like a teacup.
He longs to rest his head on the stone.
He picks it up, and the egg

of his sorrow burns and blossoms,
a living branch, with no wish to rule other trees.
A woman touches his hand,

puts a ring on his finger and weeps.
He thinks of his father, a dying king
who said, *You were two-thirds*

on your mother's side, one-third for me.
The man touches the egg in his pocket,
picks up a feather,

and rises over fields, making black trees
stand still. He doesn't know
his coat is glowing.

Missing the Owl

My Move

Our father grows old and walks slowly now,
so I let him set the pace. He says,
Soon you'll be beating me at chess. The night
is cold, and I am thinking how the force
of combinations drives his steps,
as his left foot strikes the pavement
like the weighted chess piece on stone tables
in the city park, where as a child I watched him
and the old men play. Now he drags his right foot
up as though reminding me that it's my move.
My end-game isn't good enough, I say.

It takes time, which you've got plenty of.

The winter stars are brilliant in the bitter air.
Through dark branches years are blowing.
Someday they will rise and sweep the stars
like chessmen from the edge of the sky.
Still our father walks one step ahead,
and I keep time. Under arched elm trees
in brilliant air, I make my quiet move,
do not accept his gambit.

In Our Grandma Hale's Painting, Which She Gave Me

Nothing can keep the white farmhouse
from floating in moonlit smoke from a black locomotive.

The molten orange field
in an invisible sun whose gold haystacks
can't stop glowing.

The sun, the moon, a brother and sister,
two black-and-white cows—

near one's nose, a bee
almost big as the incredulous bonnet
our Grandma's cousin Millie

wore in the asylum on Long Island.
I never wanted children, our Mom told me.

Oh white triangle of fruit trees,
oh red barn roof.

Say what you want about the Jews—
they make good family men,
said Grandma.

The place inside the barn.
Oh frozen cherry trees. Oh two white silos.

Scissors in Second Grade

He has trouble with his scissors, read my teacher's note
to our mother, as if I were an errant fawn
who had not yet learned to print his feet
exactly on construction paper.

The fault was the scissors, I thought, which went their way
through jagged red-yellow thickets, maroon zigs
and zags, umber branches, not a clear procession
of hooves in water, stepping where

they're meant to go, which would become one story
of this life. It's wayward, said my accountant father
of my handwriting, aligned not on, but precisely
above the pale blue line.

Wildfires, St. Paul Riots

In August when fireweed turned white,
and the sun hung like a poppy in smoke—
Beauty takes a beating in the streets,
I wrote, *and truth tries to do too much.*

That night the orange half-moon,
a smudge pot in funerary shadows—
now my sister says, *There's no virus,
it's a plot by the government—*

this host's an army, a throng.
Fumes and rumors fuse no sinews, bro.
George Floyd is dead, I tell her.

And the sun has the gall to come up.

American Sentences

... mercy always just turning away ...   —Rainer Maria Rilke

1

A winter tree, a rootball of ice—her six crows in six dimensions.
Even the singer who trusts his ear must see her once more
      to believe ...

Yes, we were happy, bro, she says—you know, it didn't belong to us.
When time flows backwards, I can see how memoir is reverie,
      a sieve.

Once a leaf in sunlight, now she sleeps with the moon in a
      cardboard box.
I tell my sister. She says, *I look terrible.*

2

Chloe used to find my eyeglasses for me, called me *Itchy Richie.*
Our father told us about St. Stylites who lived for years on
      his sky pole.

Mom's up there with Edith, Paul, and everyone, she says on a
      borrowed
cell phone. I've sent Mom's snapshots to her friend. They're
      yours, I say.

You shouldn't have, she says. *Down here the trees, all the doors
      are porous, bro.*

3.

It's the week of the Jessica's on 4-South; we number them 1, 2,
3—Dr. Val pounds a fist on our black center table. *Shit*. Only

time he's cursed; he charted on the wrong one. Jessica 3 tells
    me, *See*
this sketch, it's me in pieces. Hey, man I tried to find you—
    where were you?

I couldn't breathe. Why would I punch Tim in the neck? See,
    I tried to make
something beautiful like you said—see my ring-neck cat. I
    would never

do anything to hurt her. They won't let me see my little kitty.
It's not fair. I borrow your felt-tip pen. You write it on your
    white-board.

I pray for my cuz, pray at your gates. I stabbed her in the
    forearm, jabbed
my thigh with a ball point pen. No, it's easier than feeling
    nothing.

Please, call my cuz, tell her to bring my ring-neck kitten.
    You owe me, man.

4.

Blueberry summer, plum buckle at dusk—on our road, one
      coyote ...
They blossom, too, by the road, her pink Rugosa roses—
      each petal

keeps its redolence, a separate musk. Dew drops on the
      Lady's Mantle
magnify stamens. A goldfinch splashes yellow. In its blue
      dust coat,

black cloak, a Steller's jay pecks at suet. Her blue
      forget-me-not's ...
We pick blueberries, reach in the leaves for mercy slow as
      any stone.

No-see-ums: At Smith State Park

Yellow larches in October; yes, we waited
for my sister who has no phone, does not answer
her door. At least she has her own place. *Look*,
you say, focusing binoculars. Between red cliffs,
a tightrope walker with no safety rope.
One arm veers up; her other arm
swings down. Before my mother's death,
we never knew if Chloe would sign her name
at the bank. In a dream last night,
Mom teetered between constellations,
cupping two red planets in her hand.
Small as no-see-ums, she said. Now this woman
rights herself in midair. I let out my breath.
Yellow larches, red cliffs in the sun.

Poem at Age Seventy-Five

...a tattered coat upon a stick...   —*W. B. Yeats*

This off-white candle, almost cream-colored,
its inner walls an ice cave—a yellow flame
narrow at the tip. Last night we walked
down empty streets in the snow, did not speak
of flesh and what it holds. Did not say much;
as if we were the last two left on this planet
to touch each other, we clasped hands,
interlocked our fingers. I want to say
there is a flame that licks at ice and shadows.
As for this candle, well, I don't know.

High School Graduation Swing-Out

One evening in April, she's running downstairs
in a white dress, almost like a waterfall. The next day,
it's June—we're incandescent paisley in the sun,
a parade of red Impalas, Chevy Novas, tops down.
She has the poise of a mirror, as if she saw
us at our reunion fifty years later. Myron will have died
in Viet Nam. My sister will sleep with the moon
in a cardboard box. Did we laugh at our old motto,
the End of the Beginning, which we called
the Beginning of the End? It was not
supposed to be this frozen waterfall,
not that snow.

A Holding Action

—in memory of I. W.

I won't bring a Jewish child into this world
till Hitler's dead, said our father. Strange to feel affection
for this uncle I never met—wounded on an island
in the Pacific whose name we never knew, his stretcher
lugged onto a hospital triage plane that would be
shot down that same day.

In a snapshot, he stands at ease by Schofield Barracks.
Brown uniform with brass buttons. His sure-fire grin.
He had made Grandpa's mannequin store on Broome Street
into a business—the best one of us, an athlete, a swimmer,
said our father. *He fought a holding action*
that let us win.
                After the remains were shipped
to a marked grave in Lexington, Kentucky,
Dad received a compassionate leave of absence.
He wanted to call me Irving, but our Mom
did not care to name her son for the dead—
my middle name Eric as close
as we could get to *Iri*, which means *Watchful.*
Irving, I never thanked you for your gift
that bought us time, and I was born.

Shalom

—in memory of C. C.

1

How can it be, when we visit her in hospice—
"America's Got Talent" turned down low
on the TV—a man with tortoise shell glasses
twists his torso in and out of a white ring,
a toilet seat, yes, a toilet seat.
His goofy smile of wonder—we don't want to,
but we laugh. Now a nurse adjusts oxygen,
ups the morphine. Out the window, layers
of stippled clouds. Last night, you dreamt
of bears in your room. The nurse
wakes Carol, asks her religion.
If I'm anything, I'm Jewish, she says.

2

In the needle-stitch Carol has left me,
shtetl people spell out the word, *Shalom.*
The S, a green man dancing; The H,
a man and woman, hands entwined.
A, they are about to kiss. L, a Litvak
carpenter with upraised hammer.
O, an oval, two men with arched backs.
M, two lovers; their hands meet.
May she rest, *Shalom,* may she rest.

As We Walk West on Dupont Street

Behind phone wires, cloud wisps like pink-red fingers
seem to drift with us. *They're fuchsia*,
you say. Last evening on 4-South, we admitted
a frail older woman. Thelma didn't know
where she was. When I told her, she glared
at my plastic I.D. badge. That explains
a lot about *you*, she said, stubbing one finger
toward my chest.
               Under the green EXIT sign
glowing like radium, she proceeded to sit mute
by our locked double doors, blocked the entrance,
refused to go to her room. Four of us cradled her
like a gaunt peahen. *May your souls be forgiven*,
she said.
          As our charge nurse Miss Dee
gave her the injection of Ativan, we held Thelma
gently on her bed. Later, I strummed
the unit guitar, a few chords in the dark.
By our hall table, not far from our bright
nurses station, I sang "On Wings Of A Dove"
as she had asked. Now in the west, red clouds
almost like fringes—on the empty street,
we stop, and they stop, too.

On Our Thirty-Fifth Anniversary

I've chased two brown-tailed deer from your rose bush
still almost bare this morning. Past the goat shed, the first
faint haze of yellow-green, the green leaves now.
Let me give thanks for our small red house,

this love which *wasn't supposed to last,*
said my father, who was always right.
Why do you have to be right? you asked him.
I don't have to be right, he replied. *I am right.*

Before she died, my mother said, *Sing out!*
as if she knew I'd be grateful for green mazes,
fate and happenstance, a sun half-hidden,
closed buds of your azaleas this dark pink.

January 6, 2021

My friend says she was under the water between Oakland and SF
when she got the news. Her blade-thin son, his gut stopped up.

I watched security cameras on TV, the mob chasing a guard
up flights of steps, one flight at a time—he'd hold them

a few seconds and retreat. No backup. Here foothills hold
the sky and smoke boils over; the mob dukes it out with cops

in the vestibule. We ask this fire to hold us close,
scourge knife-skin at the back of our knees. My friend

wants what's righteous to write her, tell her
how to save her son. I'm hills, I'm smoke. My country

we love like smoke loves fire it escapes from.
Two placards on a goat shed for our dead friend,

one decapitated flower. Corona was a place;
now everywhere is a place that says, This isn't a virus

that runs its course. Two angels, one of vengeance,
one of flame. *I'm not you*, each cries out; *you're not me.*

Saying Evening Prayers at Our Zoom Services

A big-leaf maple glows in the sun
by the goat shed, as if its DNA knew the code
to turn carbon dioxide into oxygen.
In her hospital bed, our mother saw a world
made of red-black letters. *So beautiful,*
she said. Haven't certain Jews believed
the world was created from Hebrew
letters? This spider web on the lawn—
at online services, we say, *Adonai,*
You bring down the eyelids of evening.
Maybe, a certain white-crowned sparrow
carries our mother's name into the dark,
a missing alphabet, her sabbath of rest.

Morning Light

No, I do not think the woman in this solitary
painting by Edward Hopper has just lost her baby.
She gazes out her window, as if she knew
cold sunlight is her only child. Perhaps, the trip
she plans to take to a brook, her sunless
meadow, is one she won't return from. A choice
like seven extra months to live, but no sun.
She sings no gauzy arias; she faces down
the fish-back clouds out her bright window.
Her aches and obligations—no regrets
for trips she never took to East Hyannis,
for lids of Mason jars that came unscrewed,
for dot.com doctors in their crimson RAV4's.
Her Noels have always been for strangers,
distant kin who've come to learn
as she has, how to love, if not themselves,
then stone arches, certain wells that never....
Her white slip elicits not my longing
but this wish to know how tomorrow's
guardians may bless her unravaged face.

When a Hawk Flushes an Undulating Flock of Dunlins near Fir Island

Over a cloud-bank, lines of dunlins veer across the Sound.
When I woke in the dark this morning—the chair, the bed,
    the desk—
where were you? Now through binoculars, these wings
    slate-gray
above, gray-white below. We've seen them flash in the sun—
white, black, white—a sleeve pulled inside out, unraveling.
Over upturned stumps and floating branches in this slough,
they vanish, reappear as wind lines across gray water.
In Hebrew *ruach* means *breath, wind, spirit.*

Messenger in Early November

— in memory of J. K.

Driving past Agate Bay, I catch a glimpse
of this deer in a splotch of sun and shadow—
the brown-tail's flanks on the edge of the road
in yellow leaves, thin branches. Last May
after your death, a bear cub loped beside my car
like a lost Labrador, seemed to disappear
under my front bumper. Slamming on the brakes,
I felt no thud, heard nothing. Amazing, the cub
as if uninjured, clambered up the ditch-bank.
Only later, after your memorial, did I reread
your last poems, that black bear nosing
at your sleeping bag in the camp site
in Arizona; recalled marmots whistling
in pillow basalt near Mt. Baker; the grouse
thumping its tail near our driveway,
feasting on red hawthorn berries.
You noticed. I cannot believe you said No
to another go-round on the cancer wish machine,
you called it, completed your book, *First Stars*.
On your last hike, you raced downhill
in your wheelchair, shouting. You must
be in these sun spots, mottled shadows.
Too excellent a camouflage, my friend—
thin, flickering branches, a few gold leaves,
before all the color goes away.

Migration: You Ask Me What I Want

When flocks of snow geese gather on the low, wet fields
near Conway in mid-February, the whir of black-tipped wings,

a fire of dying constellations in my throat—their cries
not in unison, no—scattered ice floes flying home.

Missing the Owl

You have to come look right now,
she says. A Great Horned Owl in the spruce tree
by our red house—I scan layers and levels

in dark branches. Nothing; then a bough
swings up, and it's flown. At least she saw
the tufted horns, wings that open, close.

As if some beast of mercy had offered
this late chance, I gaze at the straight, gray trunk,
dead center of the tree,

then turn to her lilacs, humble bees—
now, the smell of rain.

About the Author

Missing The Owl is Richard Widerkehr's fifth book of poems. His previous books are *Night Journey* (Shanti Arts Publishing), *At the Grace Cafe* (Main Street Rag), *In the Presence of Absence* (MoonPath Press), *The Way Home* (Plain View Press). He has also authored three chapbooks and a novel, *Sedimental Journey* (Tarragon Books). His poems and stories have appeared in over one hundred publications, including *Rattle*, *Atlanta Review*, *Crab Creek Review*, *I-70 Review*, and *Verse Daily*. One of his poems was broadcast by Garrison Keillor on *Writer's Almanac*.

Widerkehr won two Hopwood first prizes for poetry at the University of Michigan, first prize for a short story at the Pacific Northwest Writers Conference, three awards in The Bridge's poetry contests, and three Sue C. Boynton Contest prizes. He worked as a teacher in the Upward Bound Program at Western Washington University and as a counselor on the mental heath unit of a hospital.

Rather than try and thank everyone, the author wishes to recommend books by the following poets: Barbara Bloom, Linda Conroy, Ryler Dustin, Patricia Hooper, Gayle Kaune, Jay Klokker, Jenifer Browne Lawrence, Gary Copeland Lilley, and Joseph Stroud. Thanks to Christine Cote for bringing out this book and, most of all, to Linda Ford for the day-to-day love that made these particular poems possible.

SHANTI ARTS

NATURE ▪ ART ▪ SPIRIT

Please visit us online
to browse our entire book catalog,
including poetry collections and fiction,
books on travel, nature, healing, art,
photography, and more.

Also take a look at our highly regarded art
and literary journal, *Still Point Arts Quarterly*,
which may be downloaded for free.

www.shantiarts.com

www.ingramcontent.com/pod-product-compliance
Lightning Source LLC
Chambersburg PA
CBHW070008100426
42741CB00012B/3157